(A)LIVE HEART

Imani Sims

SIBLING RIVALRY PRESS
LITTLE ROCK, ARKANSAS
DISTURB / ENRAPTURE

(A)live Heart
Copyright © 2016 by Imani Sims

Cover art: Flickr Commons
Author photograph by Natasha Marin
Cover design by Seth Pennington & Bryan Borland

All rights reserved. No part of this book may be reproduced or republished without written consent from the publisher, except by reviewers who may quote brief excerpts in connection with a review in a newspaper, magazine, or electronic publication; nor may any part of this book be reproduced, stored in a retrieval system, or transmitted in any form, or by any means be recorded without written consent of the publisher.

Sibling Rivalry Press, LLC
PO Box 26147
Little Rock, AR 72221

info@siblingrivalrypress.com

www.siblingrivalrypress.com

ISBN: 978-1-943977-15-4

Library of Congress Control No: 2016945232

This title is housed permanently in the Rare Books and Special Collections Vault of the Library of Congress.

First Sibling Rivalry Press Edition, October 2016

(A)LIVE HEART

11	A Ghazal for Black Girls
12	The Last Baptism
13	Before the Blood
14	Cages Never Sing
15	Roleplay
16	Threnody
17	How to Experience Resurrection
18	Aftershocks
19	Blood Caffeinated with Blues
20	In a Forest
21	Kitchen Counters and Miracle Whip
22	Aquarius
23	What of Tails and Oceans?
24	Elliott Bay: White-Capped Seas
25	Pretty Girls Don't Get Tickets
26	Consanguinity
27	Chanel No. 5
28	Soul Retrieval
30	Mo(u)rning Cup

31	For Gwendolyn Brooks' "We Real Cool"
32	Griot Tells Velvet Fragments Whole
34	Medusa Bone
35	Cobalt Tears
36	Paragon
37	What Does Jiminy Cricket Know Anyway?
38	Spitting - Image
39	Nudist Saturday
40	(Re)Spire
41	Sutured Bullet
42	Uncovered Voodoo
43	Trenchant Moon
44	Kumquat
45	little red
46	little Red
47	Silken Sulk
48	Little Red
49	After You've Made an Altar of Your Name

This is dedicated to my FGM.
The woman with a live heart.
Xoxo

A Ghazal for Black Girls

There are bones beneath the couch cushions,
Stuffed almost slouch-sugared muscle collection.

We gather in the living room: story-tell the dead
Exploits—alleged sinew sown like golden thread collection.

The answer to alphabet soup is tomato drenched underbelly,
Pork fat and Bessie, she had a name until butchered into bite-size collection.

Stomach this: a name chewed in reverse erases what memory
Our parents shape around our sounds. Take inventory: a collection.

Gather your letters to the east, know rise in every moment's ache,
(*your name here*), never satiate open mouths with soul's ripe collection.

The Last Baptism

She is more evaporated
Salt than warm water:
Crystallized residue against tub,

Faint scent of lavender
memory. Anodyne film
Suited only for ache

Of almost broken bones
And bruised skin. Lifeless
Ring, stain on porcelain.

Before the Blood

She is fissile
breast bone almost
break: ash gray

after combust. Sordid
tongue slip, thighs
parted to beckon.

Cages Never Sing

She hol(e)y kneed neon
Green tights at recess   before
The touching began. Men
Took little girl parts for devour,
Held her in their hands,
Called her their own, limp

Dove too close
To bone, bent knee pat
Pat and perch pretty bird,
She is the plumage they
Want, until she grows

Too different to fit
In their mouths, breasts
Unwanted citrus holdings,
Danger. "She will tell."

So they clip her wings.
Shade them sapphire: tie dye
Bloodline. A hunger transformed:

Their mouths stitched
In ink patterns across
Her aging breast, buckled legs
An open cage, her lovers

Piss in. A body

Now, swings on splintered
Perch. The song at
Sunset a low recant:
Elegy for neon birds.

Roleplay

She is salt lined flesh-
Open wound. Exposed bone
Ground into dust, pack
It in purse. Blow

Clouds into empty chests. She is
Mistress, ornamented headdress,

A pleasure not her own-
Orgasms of lovers dried,

At the back of throat—

She has
Always been the other
Woman, silent yes taken
Too far. Lovers' lies shape vortex

In her chest. Convince
Her insecurities safe.
Take dove-eyed softness,
And rename her pigeon:

Messenger to remind
Them of their voices. What
Woman
Doesn't want to be heard?

Threnody

She is uncarved maple,
Unstrung violin—aw—bow—
Polish, more undisturbed
Root and colored leaves.
Her body is not
Broken shards or fresh
Scent of singe, rather
Mossed limbs & limp wrists.

How to Experience Resurrection

Gather the pieces.
Lion
By the mouth.

Collect your demons,
Slay them with
Your teeth, spit

Out their bones
In reverse, so
You remember never

To chew these
Roles forward, again.
They are not

Yours. They belong
To the one
Slain by bedside

Table, bleeding into
Floor vents, staining
Carpet. Collect her

Twelfth rib, keep
It. Remind yourself
Of your sacred.

Never
    Look
        Back.

Aftershocks

There are ghosts
Between her ribs:
Tissued monsters gnawing

At the woven
Muscle, singing fault
Lines into chest:

Promise of broken
Heart, years later
She still rumbles

With disbelief, every
Time she's touched.

Blood Caffeinated with Blues

Ralph Ellison wrote an entire novel about
invisibility.

She is beginning to understand the glass.
Ghosts always return, so her ribs
keep cracking beneath the pressure.
She has become hag. Worn monster
riding Clock's tick-tocked rhythm
like steel drum sweat and matted
hair beneath headwrap. Dance
until bones shake loose. Dance
until you forget red is oxygenated

excuse for weakness. Dance your history
present.

In a Forest

Defined color within absence.
Frayed edge against wood—

She is dark spot
On white birch   :

Kitchen Counters and Miracle Whip

She has decided
To stop kneeling
At the mouths
Of others. Willing

Sacrifice for bloodied
Teeth, loud cracks
Of bone under
Pressure. She has

Decided to stop
Bleeding for those
Who whisper, call
Her midnight snack.

She is done
Clipping her soul
Short to make
Cover for the

All-ready warm.

Aquarius

She has clenched
The forgotten place
That quietly boils
Beneath her skin:
Every moment she
Dreamt she would
Ever be more
Than black girl
Twisted root forgotten
Agave lips—gourd
Bottomed succulence: silent.
She has choked
Rivers far more
Times than she
Can count, so
She considers herself

Wave slapped sand
And moonlit cheekbones.

What of Tails and Oceans?

She remembers herself
As scales, translucent
Water slick decoration

Always attached to
Skin, but today
Rainbow flaked shield

Becomes defiant declaration.

Elliott Bay White-Capped Seas

She has learned
We can control
Only as much

As any human
Can tame ocean
In mason jar

Stale sealed and
Shipped further than
Messages will carry

Her. She has
Learned we can
Only learn to

Swim or surf.

Pretty Girls Don't Get Tickets

It's funny how
pretty girls get
off with warnings,

but **black** girls
get arrested. Die
in jail cells.

When
did pretty become
skin colored sentence
steel rod stitched

to cement. But
what does it
mean to be

captive parts piled

beneath "you are
just a black
girl, mule, mammy,

pick-a-ninny, object: oppressed":
cheese grits and fried fish.

Testament to low
hung ripe fruit.

Consanguinity

She is blood
Deep ancestral chime,
Sure footed medicine

Woman, witchdoctor rune,
Winter ice against
Hidden sacrifice: Thick

Slick pussy lips:

Eternal night.

Chanel No. 5

She is bottled
Potion, pop cork.
Un-stop liquid

Rush because she
Is only good
For fluid. Never

Stored long enough
To age delicately,
Force complex flavors.

She is flat
Fee, 2.50 per
Bottle and consumed:

Quick fix, guaranteed
Hangover and dried
Cork red stain.

Soul Retrieval

You find her, coiled but unbound
Strewn across peppermint Lily field
Memory distended, ego dancing leaf
To leaf. Macrocosm arched over singular.

Strewn across peppermint Lily field
She is frozen in time. Witness
To leaf. Macrocosm arched over singular
Petal, mess of red bled into white.

She is frozen in time. Witness
Her drunken laugh produce stars.
Petal mess of red bled into white,
The sky takes on a particular darkness.

Her drunken laugh produces star
Spun sound wave aspiration.
The sky takes on a particular darkness
Under the pressure. She god

Spun sound wave aspiration
To contain the universe: one blink
Under the pressure—she god
Begins to unravel, stretch limbs

To contain the universe one blink
Serves as time. Infinite plural pattern
Begins to unravel, stretch limbs
Past recognition. Color fades.

Serves as time infinite plural pattern
Born of thirty sun revolutions brown
Past recognition. Color fades
Into mosaic world iced. Still

Born of thirty sun revolutions brown
Body, a lifetime served feminine
Into mosaic world iced still.
Survived inscribed across this wilted

Body. A lifetime served feminine
Is inferno burned ashen phoenix
Survived. Inscribed across this wilted
Garden, a duality played plain

Is inferno burned ashen. Phoenix
Lives life neon blaze
Garden: a duality played plain
Is apologetic existence. She
Never wanted this. Infinite

Lives. Life neon blaze
Tail feather swung wide
Never wanted this infinite
Bow of submission—dismiss.

Tail feather swung wide
Memory distended, ego dancing leaf
Bow of submission dismiss.
You find her, coiled but unbound.

Mo(u)rning Cup

She is rock
Sugar tang hibiscus:
Full bloom body
And effervescent POP.

For Gwendolyn Brooks' "We Real Cool"

We keep our pieces
Like coin: shiny bubblegum
Pop cornerstore after thought.

Jaywalk at midnight follow
The light because salvation
Has always been simple: _____ .

Griot Tells Velvet Fragments Whole

Born into Faith (n.):
She has learned
to hide tears
in the basin
beside her bed. It has never been okay for black woman to cry.
{unspoken covenant.}

She has never
felt more sure
of her tears
worthy. Though black   woman only wonder
when to return to stone.

She has always
wanted Medusa[1] for
lover, ugliness is
more suitable for   black woman want and slick desire.

She desires a
life foundation and
letters too secret
to speak. Keep   womanhood safe from unwanted passengers.

She is the
only rider on
this ferried existence,
permanent transport for   black.woman.slick.safe.
                                    {Red.Velvet.Vulva.}

---

[1] "'Except,' she said, in a whisper, 'if you are from Africa you recognize Medusa's wings as the wings of Egypt, and you recognize the head of Medusa as the head of Africa; and what you realize you are seeing is the Western world's memorialization of that period in prehistory when the white male world of Greece decapitated and destroyed the black female Goddess/Mother tradition and culture of Africa.'"
-Alice Walker, *The Temple of My Familiar*

Raised a Gentle Lamb (v.):
She is broken wish
Bone and scattered meat:
The leftovers—refrigerated ziplock
Storage bag, discarded cornbread
Stuffing. Separated fragments
Others can enjoy, she
Far from home.

Labeled Rock (adj.):
She was never delicate
Stringed gossamer all lace
And no regrets.

Her eyes will never
Surrender.

Medusa Bone

Scraped knuckle
Ferocious,
Down on all fours,

A weight: the cocked gun,
Smoke barrel death as
Stretched limbs to skyline,

Block bullet,
Heart: has always been stone,
Impenetrable,

Original medusa, turned goddess,
All snaked ventricles swinging
Between ribs,

Writhing fortress.

Dance limbed knowledge,
History latent in marrow.

Listen,

As sound waves
Crack your medusa

And   shake free   bone.

Cobalt Tears

She wakes:
7 layers in—
A prayer she never
Told anyone scripted to thighs
Like menstrual blood stained panties days
Old. Dry. Pleading cotton surrender. She. More
Amber stain and forgotten swipe. Filigree
Wounds all floral scent—ooze.
A body. Distinct mourn,
Empty cobalt tears,
Sutured stuck.
Sunflower.

Paragon

Coal.
Mistaken

Unapologetic digested diamond:
She has tasted heat.
Emerged covered
In soot, burned bone.

She has learned to
Breathe through the flames.

What Does Jiminy Cricket Know Anyway?

She feels as
Though her right
To be anything

Other than villain
Has been stolen.
All parts of

Her have been
Warped into trigger:
Gun smoke and

Last breath silence.
She has become
The last thing

People see before
Scarlet red. She
Never wanted this

Broken bone and
Bloody mess. She
Never wanted spatter

Patterns on nightgowns
Or silent wishes
For death.

Spitting - Image

*... our mothers are the ones who teach us about the cycles of life
as our first spiritual teachers ...*

– The Moon Woman

She has decided
That she will
Circumvent the notion

Of her mother's
Desperation and send
Blood bent bone

T u m b l i n g
                        T u m b l i n g
                                              Out.

Nudist Saturday

Sometimes she forgets
Her body is
More than skin
And teeth bone.

Today, she feels
As though she
Is all sacred
Si(gh)te and drench.

(Re)Spire

She has not inhaled this deeply
since the day she decided to double
shot of whiskey and fries
down I-5, no plans and ketchup
stains on holey jeans, a
close friend in the driver's seat.

In fact: she does not know
if deep properly describes

this over oxygenated hum
lowering her senses into ecstasy.
To break up with a dying lover
is the only way to regain breath,
so she sits close to the window
and awaits the perfect moment
to ex[pand].

Sutured Bullet

She has, above all else,
Become martial law: sutured

Bullet powder clouds. blood.
How else would her bones discover

Authentic structure: unhinged cap
And holy ghost. white.

Uncovered Voodoo

She has always been
God. Stamped behind third
Eye lid. Uncovered voodoo whispers

Turn white men
To stone: medusa.

Earth, unbound woman
Too tall for common
Ground.

Trenchant Moon

She has never seen decorative horns
rise from thick earth moon
quite like the ox shudder
of a distant truth. Her bones
become mirrors, they crack open,
shake the dust loose. Mend
has never been so simple:
open. release. close. suture. surrender.

KUMQUAT

She is hard rind
slow citrus burst—seed:
unflowered bud, dry smoke
high, rolling laughter/Peach.

LITTLE RED

She is chest
full of fists
and uninterrupted tears
for organs, body

shook wails wear
her like shroud:
hooded story no
wolf has ever

read.

little Red

She wonders if
She will become
Less little > more

Red re(a)ds
Star spangled bodies
Like year long

Horoscopes splattered across
The only sky
She has ever

Known, every wrinkle
A galaxy discovered
By her touch.

Silken Sulk

She thought Red
was less Alice
and forgotten rabbit
foot, but Red
whips meringue
like wonder transport
to lands where vanilla
wafers are staple
food for survival
and ghosts lurk
silken sulk whisper
in the bathroom.

Little Red

Red's real name
Is Allegrah, but
She never tells

Anyone because hood
Always comes first.
She wishes away

On summer days
That she could
Be al(l) leg & RAH!

After You've Made an Altar of Your Name

Split your chest a six fingered hand, cradle
Repurposed syllables, fan them back into soul,
All clear the air sage and woody smoke.

Light honey scented candle, swallow your letters
Whole. Spell them back after 24 hour digest,
Let your tongue taste bitter, sour, salty, sweet.

Sweat your soul neon green, dance to the curves
Your sound bounces back, hail percussion
And bass in gut, roll body upward.

Heft your breath to shadowed perspire
Night walls, stand erect, let stars
bear witness of self born infinite.

About the Poet

Imani Sims lives in Seattle, Washington, where she drinks gallons of chai tea on rainy Saturdays plotting new ways to share her story and make room for the Queer Woman of Color narrative. She spun her first performance poem at the age of fourteen. Since then, she has developed an infinitely rippling love for poetry in all of its forms. She believes in the healing power of words and the transformational nuance of the human story. Imani works to empower youth and adults through various writing courses and interdisciplinary shows. She sings while doing everything but writing and loves to create meals in the kitchen. She is a Board Member for Earth Pearl Collective, a non-profit dedicated to creating safe spaces for queer black womyn to be empowered through artistic collaborations, social events, and educational workshops.

About the Press

Sibling Rivalry Press is an independent press based in Little Rock, Arkansas. It is a sponsored project of Fractured Atlas, a nonprofit arts service organization. Contributions to support the operations of Sibling Rivalry Press are tax-deductible to the extent permitted by law, and your donations will directly assist in the publication of work that disturbs and enraptures. To contribute to the publication of more books like this one, please visit our website and click *donate*.

www.ingramcontent.com/pod-product-compliance
Lightning Source LLC
Chambersburg PA
CBHW060222050426
42446CB00013B/3142